ALMOST HOME

Les Bernstein

Berkana Publications
Sebastopol, CA

ALMOST HOME

ISBN: 979-8-9923023-4-9

Published by:

    Berkana Publications

    Sebastopol CA 95472 USA

Author's websites and contact information:

    lessieb13@yahoo.com

Cover image: photo by Les Bernstein

Printed in the United States of America

other books written or edited by Les Bernstein

Poetry:

Borderland
Naked Little Creatures
Amid the Din
Loose Magic

Anthologies:

The Smalls: Selections from the 2025 CA Writer Club
Vision and Verse 2024: A Fusion of Art, Photography, Prose and Poetry
One Day: Redwood Writers 2024 Poetry Anthology
Phases: Redwood Writers 2023 Poetry Anthology
Crossroads: Redwood Writers 2022 Poetry Anthology
Beyond Distance: Redwood Writers 2021 Poetry Anthology
And Yet: Redwood Writers 2020 Poetry Anthology
Crow: Redwood Writers 2019 Poetry Anthology
Phoenix: Redwood Writers 2018 Poetry Anthology
Rock Paper Scissors: 2018 Marin Poetry Center High School Anthology

For Irving William Bernstein
May 17, 1943 – May 11, 2020
and my family

Table of Contents

Almost Home

this undiminishable journey
is the destination
from wonder into wonder
beginning and beginning again

The Ordinary

unlike a gibbous moon
a sunrise of wonder
with undertones of melancholy
can shadow to darkness

as a rosary of days disperse
an astonishment of existence
hits most of the expected beats
gives pulse to unbidden miracles

between no more and not yet
a story heeds to life's hues
happiness and sorrow
sparkling facets of the same gem

In Defense of Awe

in an unpredictable journey
no angels observe
the apple returning to the tree

an overstocked pantry of mind
performs daily mercies
mitigates the hard questions

yet a spinning earth hangs in endless sky
orbited by numberless possible worlds
our neurons strive to fashion meaning

change will come to pass
calling us home
luminous and humbled

Excalibur

someplace in the here
where we live
an autumn leaf of a woman
tripoded with an aluminum cane
asks if I live nearby

I live mostly in my head
adjusting memories
inventing futures
conversing with ghosts
little use for bright certainty

orbited by numberless impossibilities
she asks where to buy
a battery for her watch
her time has stopped
and is running out

I say pharmacy
for chemistry and chance
we smile
leaning on her cane
she inches her stooped way

I wish I had an answer
for all the outwardly ordinary details
that make up a life
but my sword
is still stuck in the stone

I am as Old as my Dog

food is of no interest
car rides do not matter
tail does not wag
has an enlarged heart
sleeps most of the day
arthritis and cataracts
diabetic and deaf
that time is coming
a compassionate shot
I will ask for one too

Halfway House

the gas burner is left on
glasses cannot be found
no separation of wash
all their clothes pink and grey

they forget their pills
dad drives at abnormal speed
mom too tired to cook
makes tuna nightly

their neurons weave
bits and bobs
a noble struggle
in delicate circuitry

stunned by their quotidian
I make a home for my parents
a paucity of self-sufficiency
runs a low wattage current

in my house
they allow to be smoothly settled
regain control and certainty
find their glasses

a sky above
a sky below
the imps of aging
relocate us all

Sherlie

my mother left an envelope for me
it contained a list of contents to be disbursed
rings to my daughters
watch to my son
thimble collection to a grandchild
charm bracelet to oldest granddaughter
crocheted doilies for my daughter-in-law
miniatures of German Shepherds for a grandson
her framed photo of George and Laura Bush
to my democrat husband
the list went on
filled with the remains of days
ephemera etc.
at the end of this catalog
she wrote
"you were a good child... no complaints"
leaving me with
an excellent Yelp review
and a geriatric cat

Night's Journey into Day

the night before a rose scent
permeated our dark quiet home
they came for her in the afternoon
with a large zip plastic bag
a tag for her toe
a gurney for the trip
three hours before
she had asked for her shoes
what was it that called to her
beckoned her to be somewhere else
did she wish to follow the scent
did she leave head-first
or was it her shoeless feet

Atom and Dust

in the beginning he said
this diagnosis is only words
because he was magical
we believed he would be well
now on the night table
on his side of the bed
there is a box
and he is in it

storms dense with incident
tore thru our lives
time moved in one direction
demanded its due
yet sun moon stars
performed everyday miracles

we try to live
this unpredictable journey
between atom and dust
with our whole hearts
anyway

Anniversary

Spruce is an elegant restaurant
with white linen tablecloths
and red velvet banquettes
he's dying from pancreatic cancer
and wants to take me for lunch
so off we go
he can barely eat
mostly doesn't
he wants me to drink champagne
he wants me to have the lobster salad
yes ok ...I'll order it
it comes with a black hair in it
I say nothing
I smile at the waiter
I eat around it
52 years
there will not be 53

I Probably Should Just Tell You

the work of mourning
runs on heartbeats
pulls against slow storms
and gathering squalls

survival's ticking clock
sealed in itself
has hushed auspices
and dimming lights

you slipped soundlessly
the liminal bounds of us
settled into the soft cushion
of different gardens

in our tender universe
we were simply here
and I should have paid
more attention

The Lamb Chop Grief Spiral

without nuance
it started when the butcher asked
how many lamb chops
too embarrassed to say
just two
a pathetic number
so incomplete
yet fully realized
I say four

I tell myself
each person who is stuck in the past
is stuck alone
the only valid tense is the present
I say there is a singularity
where all is one
and here
in brown paper
are the lamb chops

there was a time
dinner was shared
continuing is neither
an ethical victory
nor a noble failure

in grief's own cathedral
this now
is my only destination
what should I do on my stay here
I pick up the fork and knife
and eat

Passage

below a placid surface
of sunny yellow pursuit
there lies a human story
a narrative to provide order

fragile as a soap bubble
hope glistens and floats
gambles with the quotidian
presumes an expected future

in a world of rising sea levels
and voracious viruses
industrial strength endeavors
cannot promise safety

between wish and substance
chance is a confounding destination
made of straw and sticks
uncharted and unbridgeable

Solastalgia

in a confinement of self
and a far-off country of dream
I think I keep seeing you
I see you everywhere

we had wax wings
a common metaphor
of earnest self-importance
melting near a cold star

a family gathers smiling
in a photo not yet sepia
a routine document
someone not yet missing

what is past remains present
my heart is on the outside
how can I be homesick
while being home

Caesura

in the limits of human existence
sorrow's own enclosure
cannot communion
beyond the sky

the season of your passing
is a newly charted world
awash in dingy colors
widening the hollows

this unbreachable space
completes the aftermath
removes without absence
its silence so loud

it is said only wolves
hear the stars

How to Break Bread

start with ruddy optimism
mix yeast with water
flour with oil
wood spoon hard
grease bowl
entomb mass
towel to shroud
wait for resurrection
time to punch it silly
re-shroud
leave in warm spot to shrive
wash with debilitated egg
bake with impermanence and time
much will happen
remove from oven
set aside
for knife
and prayer

Lost in Space

suspended amid galaxies
the phenomena
of birth and death
defy explanation

the secret of existence
is guarded closely
dwells cozily
in the darkness of space

a weighty blanket of certainty
pacifies the unknowable
makes in marrow and mind
enigma comfortable

running an anemic current
belief is a low wattage delusion
reliable as a shooting star
flashing to nowhere

Bioluminescence

without celestial applause
we assemble in earthly ritual
an origami of belief folds and unfolds
a predicament of being human

lack of perspective
designed by assumption
makes conviction almost reliable
embraces consoling conclusions

life's living still shimmers
with shiny cluelessness
unanswerable questions linger
in numberless suppositions

lifelong enigmas enter
a vestibule of certainty
absenting from investigating
another holy now

Mammals

What the caterpillar calls the end,
the rest of the world calls a butterfly.
                                        —Lao Tzu

in the loom of imagination
milestones are woven
life-force devoted to a self
is entombed in ego

humans are the only mammals
with advanced knowledge of death
time dense with incident
moves only in one direction

as the sweep of histories
fall to a starker reckoning
we strive for meaning
we settle for legacy

we may linger in dreams
but still transmogrify too soon

Feeling Very Superstitious

don't
spill the salt
break the mirror
open umbrellas indoors
walk under ladders
put the hat on bed
step on the crack
get a black cat

never
forget to
whistle past cemeteries
cross your fingers
turn thrice and spit
knock twice on wood
and all should be good

these antidotes
are all in your head
most likely they are
something you've read
I promise you
you are being led

continued on next page

as for now
it is fair to say
it is all okay
you have not
dropped dead
so far today

A Questionable Philosophical Approach to Nature

Buddhism

this morning
I walked a Daddy Long Legs
out of my house
screaming
me
not the
Daddy Long Legs
does a spider
have buddha nature

Nihilism

it came too close
all eight legs
I took off my shoe
I apologized
I smushed it
screaming
me
not the …
well… you know

Today's News

in a paradise of mediocrity
glaciers are melting
with the burn of indifference
sea levels rise

a narrative of complacency
and no connecting of dots
is sure to return our dust
to an apathetic universe

is it true
that all we have accomplished
is just another age
of uncertain consequences

despots may lay claim to lands
as if human ownership is possible
they will come and go
taking nothing with their passing

Autumnal Equinox

dark so early
brackets the mood

a table set for one
suggests the absent

a gumbo of loss
made to be devoured

anhedonia mixed with tedium
seasoned with unease

Without Myth or Fable

made of straw and sticks
the outwardly ordinary details
that make up a life
huddle around the thieving nature of time

as part of this journey
it comes to pass
but never comes to stay
we must return our stardust

yet the holy moment of now
glimmers with bright certainty
that the living hearth of consciousness
is more than chemistry and chance

Before Begatting Began

with all its howling mistakes
and some sublimity intact
the repetition of existence
with its generalities
and its particulars
shuffles along

trued by circumstance
a paucity of perspective
with sure-footed uncertainty
creates faulty assumptions
makes conviction almost reliable

unanswerable questions linger
enter the waiting room of belief
before begat begat begat
the big bang?
are you sure

The Poem has a Chance to Speak for Itself

I am a solo industry
called onward by spirits
I stir and wake infrequently
provoked by happenstance
overseen by muses moved
by inaudible symphonies

within a sacred geometry
I am indisputably alive
percolating with tenderness
trying to capture
the enormous once

I can make you spark
with knowing sighs and nods
remind you of your original voice
guide travel to the secret spring
of one's truest nature

it is I who is placed
on a white page void
sent out for perusal
at times more absorbed
than understood
either way it is I
who baffle
the omnipresent emissaries
of criticism and doubt

Yahrzeit

it is your day today
I leave the windows closed
and watch the leaves scatter
and remember the sun

I know the moment
time slithered away
that day unlike all others
tangling into a hard knot

I will light a candle
to chaperone my way
to toggle between
here and nowhere

it is fall again
you inhabit the wind
while terrestrial business
continues
as if nothing changed

Yahrzeit is the anniversary of a death marked by burning a candle

Acknowledgements

Many thanks to the editors of the publications in which these poems first appeared, often and earlier version, as … I cannot keep from editing even after publication.

A Questionable Approach...	Ranger Literary Magazine
Almost Home	Just So Literary Magazine
Anniversary	Bronze Bird Book
Atom and Dust	Just So Literary Magazine
Autumnal Equinox	Little Something Press
Before Begatting Began	Stray Branch Literary Magazine
Bioluminescence	Literary Times
Caesura	Stray Branch Literary Magazine
Excalibur	Bethlehem Roundtable
Feeling Very Superstitious	The Siren's Call
Halfway House	Chiron Review
How to Break Bread	Paradox Literary Magazine
I am as Old as my Dog	One Day
I Probably Should Just Tell You	Chiron Review
In Defense of Awe	Just So Literary Magazine
The Lamb Chop Grief Spiral	Gunpowder Press
Solastalgia	Last Stanza
Without Myth or Fable	Poetically Magazine
Yahrzeit	Voice of Israel

Les Bernstein is an award-winning poet and anthologist whose poems have appeared in journals and anthologies in the United States and internationally. Her full-length book, *Loose Magic* was reviewed by the Los Angeles Review of Books and is available on Amazon. Les lives in Mill Valley, California with her enormous family.

www.ingramcontent.com/pod-product-compliance
Lightning Source LLC
Chambersburg PA
CBHW051601120626
46551CB00013B/1613